HERITAGE VILLAGE CHURCH

The Story Of People That Love

JIM & TAMMY BAKKER

Present The Ministries Of Heritage Village Church

©1986 Heritage Village Church and Missionary Fellowship, Inc.

ISBN: 0-912275-05-7

Photography by the photographers of Heritage Village Church; Bill Ross, West Light, Canoga Park, California; Phil Aull Studios, Charlotte, North Carolina.

Cover photography by Phil Aull Studios.

Design by Fortunato Aglialoro, Toronto, Canada, and the design staff of Heritage Village Church.

Editorial copy by staff writers of Heritage Village Church.

Quotations from *The Living Bible* (TLB) and from *The New International Version* (NIV) by courtesy of Tyndale House Publishers and The Zondervan Corporation respectively.

Produced by Boulton Publishing Services Inc., Toronto, Canada.

Printed in Hong Kong by Scanner Art Services Inc., Toronto, Canada.

Welcome to
Heritage Village Church!

God loves you, He really does!

Jim + Tammy Bakker

I *was glad when they said unto me, Let us go*
into the house of the Lord.

PSALM 122:1, KJV

Sunday morning worship service in the Heritage Village Church sanctuary.

Thou shalt love the Lord thy God with all thy heart, and with all thy soul, and with all thy mind.

This is the first and great commandment.

And the second is like unto it,

Thou shalt love thy neighbour as thyself.

On these two commandments hang all the law and the prophets.

MATTHEW 22:37-40 KJV

Hall of Agreement **(opposite)** *in the Heritage Grand Ministry Center.*

Again I say unto you, That if two of you shall agree on earth as touching anything that they shall ask, it shall be done for them of my Father which is in heaven

Matthew 18:19

*A*nd upon this rock I will build my church;
and the gates of hell shall not prevail against it.

MATTHEW 16:18 KJV

This book is about a church, a Christian church that is a spiritual home to thousands and that brings hope and inspiration to millions. It is a vibrant, growing church with many missionary activities, meeting a broad spectrum of human needs. It is traditional, even orthodox, in its beliefs and purposes, carrying on the work of God in modern America, taking on the forms and language and skills of this one particular moment in history.

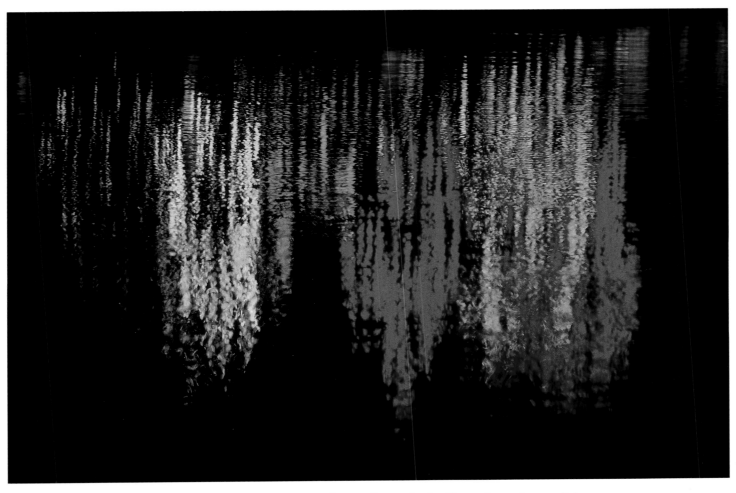

Reflections at Lake Heritage **(above)**. *Prayer in the Upper Room* **(opposite)**.

But first, what *is* a church? Not just a building. Not just a ritual, not just a set of dogmas, not just an institution or a hierarchy. Jesus said, ''Where two or three are gathered together in My Name there am I in the midst of them.'' The Christian church is an extended family under God, a community of souls. Heritage Village Church shows that the church can be all-encompassing, not just a part or a compartment of life, but life itself, all of life, with nothing left out. And this, we believe, is how Jesus intended His church to be.

The Heritage Grand Ministry Center: a place for the whole family.

The Christian lives within the church, within the timeless community of the Holy Spirit. Heritage Village Church *is making that come true* for a local congregation of thousands, *has set that as an aim* before a television congregation of millions, and enlists its own best efforts and the most advanced technologies to carry that ideal around the world.

Throughout history the Christian church has been strongest when men and women lived out their lives within the context of the church, when daily life in all its aspects was imbued with the Holy Spirit. But we do not live in the Mediterranean world of the Early Fathers, nor in the Europe of the Middle Ages, nor in the England of the great reforming missionaries—we live in America on the eve of the 21st Century.

We have modern comfortably-equipped facilities for our members, visitors, residents and volunteers; campgrounds that equal the best standards state or recreational parks can provide; homes for those who come to live in our community and for the elderly who come to find a new lease on life in a Christian environment. Our lodging accommodations, restaurants, shops and recreational facilities offer all the enjoyment to which our guests and congregations are *entitled*—without any of the dross that mars the meeting places of the secular world.

These facilities are an essential, integral part of our missionary work. We must speak to the people of our own time. If there is a better way of doing something then we must go for the better way.

Jesus calls us to be "fishers of men." In a day when evils all around us are trying to ensnare our children and our youth, we have determined in our hearts to build a place so attractive to the family that corrupting and destructive enticements lose their appeal.

Jesus said, "I am come that they might have life, and that they might have it more abundantly." The Christian life is a joyful life. It is a life of fellowship, of sharing in gladness. That is why we have celebrations, flowered parklands, singers and musicians. We believe the God we serve deserves our very best. These surroundings are the best we can create to provide a joyful setting for God's work and God's people.

If there is a "bottom line" in the Christian faith, it is love. God *is* love. God is a God of restoration. Our ministry focuses on that simple, central truth. Around that cornerstone all the work of the Kingdom will fall into place.

Horses graze near the Welcome Center at Heritage USA.

What, in practical, tangible social terms, does all that mean? God is more than loving words alone. He is love in action. So we care for the sick and the needy. We bring comfort and help to the prisoners. We bring companionship to the lonely. We save young mothers and their babies from the horrors of abortion. We help to restore the sacred ties of marriage. We offer time and the chance of healing to those who have broken their lives on drugs. We preach the Good News to the world.

In a hundred ways we work to bring back into American life that sacred awareness that every individual has a unique, eternal value. Our nation was founded on that awareness, yet millions around us today are desolate because they do not know whether they have any real purpose or value at all. Heritage Village Church exists to show them that yes, there is meaning, yes, they do have worth, yes, there *is* love, in them, and around them, revealed through the ministry of Jesus Christ. Here, now, in America, in this year of grace, God reigns through His power of love.

The children of the Heritage Village Church **(opposite).**

*B*ut ye are a chosen generation, a royal priesthood,
an holy nation, a peculiar people; that ye should
shew forth the praises of him who hath called you
out of darkness into marvellous light.

I PETER 2:9 KJV

*T*he ever-growing local congregation at the Heritage Village Church reflects the makeup of our worldwide family...a fellowship of believers from every denominational and cultural background, united in purpose and heart, assembled in one accord.

*Pastor Bakker serves communion **(above)** and ministers to the congregation **(opposite)**.*

*Ye have not chosen me, but I have chosen
you, and ordained you, that ye should go and
bring forth fruit, and that your fruit should
remain: that whatsoever ye shall ask of the
Father in my name, he may give it you.*

JOHN 15:16 KJV

As pastor of Heritage Village Church, the Reverend James O. Bakker shoulders responsibility "...for the equipping of the saints for the work of the ministry." Under his leadership, Heritage Village Church provides a full scope of programs and services to meet the needs of the congregation and the surrounding community.

Pastor Bakker brings to Heritage Village Church a wealth of experience, academic credentials and, most important of all, a heart of compassion. Praying for the sick, providing for the needy and giving shelter to the homeless, are all expressions of his commitment to offer a message of hope and love to a hurting world. A quarter-century of full-time ministry to the church universal has intensified Jim Bakker's love for God and humanity.

Each Lord's day, the mysteries of the Gospel are revealed and made plain through Pastor Bakker's anointed preaching. An unrelenting commitment to reach the world for Jesus Christ is never more evident than when this dedicated pastor ministers to his local congregation.

Pastor Bakker ministers to the television congregation.

22

For we preach not ourselves, but Christ Jesus the Lord ...

II CORINTHIANS 4:5 KJV

The role of the senior pastor extends far beyond the pulpit and includes a multitude of ministerial duties. In his study (left), Pastor Bakker attends to his correspondence with his staff and (right) offers leadership and direction during an executive planning session.

The Bakker family **(above)** *in l906 photo with Grandfather Bakker pictured second from left in the back row and inset. Jim Bakker* **(below)**, *age six months.*

I *have chosen you...*

JOHN 15:16 KJV

A zealous grandfather, a devoted grandmother and faithful parents gave Jim Bakker a heritage of evangelistic zeal and inspired in him a loving concern for all people.

His grandfather, Joe Bakker, founded and helped build the first Assembly of God Church in Muskegon, Michigan, in 1923. Grandfather Bakker's goal in life was to take the Gospel to foreign lands, but he never left his local area and died with a sense of frustration because he thought that he had failed in his mission to reach the world for Christ. He never lived to see the seed that he had planted flourish through his grandson and the ministry of Heritage Village Church, an Assemblies of God Church founded in Charlotte, North Carolina, fifty years after Grandfather Bakker founded the church in Muskegon.

24

Creston Gospel Tabernacle, founded by Jim's Grandfather Bakker. Jim's family helped build this structure by hand, and grandparents on both sides of his family were charter members. Jim's parents (below), Raleigh and Furnia Bakker, at their home in Mulberry Village at Heritage USA.

When Jim sometimes found his Pentecostal upbringing difficult to understand, Grandma Irwin was always there to encourage, to love and to listen. Church leadership over three generations handed on to Jim a profound appreciation for the ministry of the local church...

"When I was growing up, church was the center of my life. My church taught me that with faith I could do anything—and I believed it!

"As a child, I learned how to lay tile as I worked side by side with my father and other members of the congregation as we built our church...and I have been involved with building churches ever since."

In high school, a caring teacher instilled self-confidence in a timid young man, and a traumatic accident brought about Jim's total commitment to Christ. By the time he graduated, he had set aside earlier plans to become a journalist in favor of following God's calling and he enrolled in North Central Bible College. From the very beginning of his training, Jim

confessed to his classmates his dream of fulfilling the Great Commission of Matthew 28:19, to win the world for Jesus.

Meanwhile, in the small, paper-mill town of International Falls, Minnesota, God was preparing Tammy Faye LaValley for her life-long role in world evangelism.

Tammy was the eldest of eight children. Her love for music was instilled and nurtured by a mother who often gathered her brood around the piano and taught them the joy of praising God in song. Tammy began her singing career at the age of three, appearing before enthusiastic and appreciative church audiences.

A strong Christian heritage was passed on to Tammy by her mother, Rachel, who taught her a simple trusting faith in Jesus, and by Grandma Fairchild, her "best friend," who taught her the delight and joy of serving Jesus, and by Aunt Gin, who taught her to work hard and to take pride in all her work.

Jim and Tammy (above) ride the train to Minneapolis; photo taken only a few months before their marriage in 1961. The Bakkers pose (below) with a congregation in Falling Waters, West Virginia (1962).

As her spiritual commitment and keen sensitivity to the Holy Spirit deepened throughout her teenage years, Tammy felt an intense call to devote her life to full-time ministry. Unsure of where this call might lead, Tammy decided that Bible school would be the first step of preparation. With Grandma's blessing and Aunt Gin's encouragement, a dream came true. In the fall of 1960, Tammy LaValley enrolled at North Central Bible College, where she met and fell in love with Jim Bakker.

On April 1 of the following year they were married in a small, private ceremony in the prayer chapel of the church they attended in Minneapolis. Marriage intensified their vision and strengthened their commitment to a lifetime of service together.

*The young evangelist **(left)** and his devoted wife, Tammy **(below)**. Jim and Tammy with their family of puppets featured on CBN's "Jim and Tammy Show" **(bottom left)**.*

27

Four generations: *(left to right)* Tammy's mother Rachel, Tammy, Grandma Fairchild and Jamie Charles. *(opposite)* Tammy Faye Bakker.

Jim and Tammy's worldwide ministry began in a small way with faithful preaching in rural churches. For four years, they traveled throughout the southeastern United States, preaching at revival meetings and holding children's crusades. Having fulfilled the necessary requirements and having been approved by the Assemblies of God, Pastor Bakker qualified and was ordained as a minister on April 29, 1964, in Dunn, North Carolina.

Because of their effective and innovative ministry to children, the Bakkers were recommended to Pat Robertson, to create a children's program for the then-fledgling Christian Broadcasting Network.

Already in Jim's heart there was the vision of a Christian television variety program. During their years of on-the-road evangelism, Jim and Tammy would often return home late at night and hope to relax in front of the television set. Instead, having just come from the holy atmosphere of a stirring revival meeting, they would be shocked by the lewd and inane entertainment offered on late-night television. In Pastor Bakker's heart was a dream of creating a program that would uplift Christians and glorify God, instead of a "typical" religious program with loud preaching directed at an immense unseen congregation. Jim's dream was to create an intimate one-to-one format that would offer viewers a soothing, uplifting alternative to secular television.

This was the beginning of the "Christian talk show" concept, and on November 28, 1966, Jim's dream became a reality when he hosted the first *700 Club* broadcast.

For the next eight years, God used Jim and Tammy to help build the foundation of Christian television ministry at CBN and elsewhere throughout the country. Through a series of God-ordained circumstances, Jim and Tammy arrived in Charlotte, North Carolina, to found and establish the ministry of Heritage Village Church and the PTL Television Network.

Through the tireless labor of Jim, Tammy and a small staff who shared their vision, an empty furniture store was transformed into a "House of God" for proclaiming the Gospel. Together, they built a chapel by hand in the center, as a meeting place of prayer. This became the heart of the ministry. The daily two-hour television program proclaimed God's love and invited viewers to pray with volunteer counselors on the 24-hour-a-day prayer phones.

The warmth, the testimonies, and the simple message of God's love proclaimed by Jim and Tammy Bakker, swept the country as local television stations across America began broadcasting the program.

The purchase and construction of Heritage Village and Bruton Parish Church Studio, PTL's first church home, fulfilled Jim Bakker's dream for a place of beauty, excellence and Christian heritage for God's people. Only the Lord could have foreseen the ensuing growth, estimated by experts at 7,000 percent within the next eighteen months. During that same period more than 100 new television stations began airing the broadcast; the staff doubled, then quadrupled; the first-ever private satellite license was issued to PTL; a Spanish version of PTL was born to reach the Spanish-speaking world; hundreds of thousands of visitors came to Heritage Village; and

Taping the daily "Jim and Tammy TV Ministry Hour" **(above)** *at the church's broadcast studio. Directing the live broadcast* **(below)** *from the control room.* **(opposite)** *Bruton Parish, PTL's first church home.*

The World Outreach Center (above), where the main offices of the worldwide ministry of Heritage Village Church are housed. Main lobby (left) of the World Outreach Center.

thousands of calls for prayer poured into the phone lines daily. Pastor Bakker's vision of reaching the whole world for Christ stood on the verge of realization, but the 25-acre Heritage Village site was inadequate for such a goal.

Heritage USA, the place God chose for the fulfillment of Jim Bakker's greatest dream, was begun on his birthday, January 2, 1978. With his pastoral staff, he laid a master plan for a 21st-Century ministry of world evangelism on the four square mile site, designed to equip believers for total Christian living. Out of this natural

"Musical Heritage USA," a lively presentation of Gospel and folk music, being performed in the 3,500 seat outdoor Amphitheatre during the summer months.

wilderness a beautiful 400-unit campground was created, along with an outdoor church and camp meeting amphitheater, teaching and recreation facilities and a new office center to serve as world headquarters for the ministry.

However, even more facilities were needed immediately—an expanded church complex with space for education, prayer and counseling, a Bible-centered school for hands-on training in world evangelism, television production studios, suitable retreat lodging for members and visitors, and additional permanent housing for church staff and volunteers. In the face of severe opposition and unrelenting criticism, the task seemed overwhelming. But again and again, as Pastor Bakker and the church prayed, God sovereignly guided them to victory against gigantic odds.

Today Heritage Village Church has the capability to reach one billion people worldwide. Yet Jim's vision and calling continue, as the church labors to fulfill God's mission and divine promise.

Fellow elders, this is my plea to you: Feed the flock of God; care for it willingly...lead them by your good example...your reward will be a never-ending share in his glory and honor.

I PETER 5:1-4 TLB

The Heritage Village Church Board of Directors is comprised of distinguished men and women, experienced, respected and proven in leadership. They lend their collective wisdom and spiritual insight to give guidance in administering the many aspects of God's Work.

DR. RICHARD W. DORTCH, Executive Director, Heritage Village Church and Missionary Fellowship

Pastor Dortch, co-pastor, board member and executive director of Heritage Village Church, has been recognized as a gifted leader, preacher and international spokesman.

Rev. Dortch has pastored churches throughout the United States and served as a missionary and Field Fellowship Secretary for the Assemblies of God in Europe. He was President of Emmanuel Bible Institute in Brussels, Belgium, and also founder and president of three Christian radio stations in Illinois. In addition, for fourteen years he served on the highest elective body of the Assemblies of God as an Executive Presbyter. He also served as State Superintendent of the Assemblies of God in Illinois for thirteen years. He is recognized as a lifelong overseer in the Assemblies of God fellowship, which numbers fourteen-million members worldwide. For five years he was a member of the Board of Directors of the Heritage Village Church, prior to assuming his

present position as co-pastor.

"I see great periods of growth ahead for PTL," says Pastor Dortch, "as our inspiration stays fresh, our spontaneity stays alive and our growth is guided in wisdom to maturity. I thank God for Pastor Jim Bakker's vision to do more than institutionalize. His desire is to keep our ministry in touch with God!"

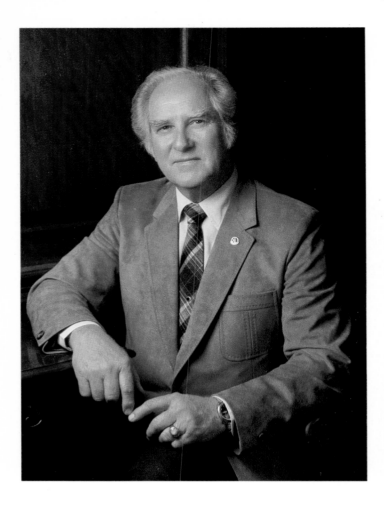

A.T. LAWING, JR., Founder, Charlotte Oil and Equipment Company, Charlotte, North Carolina

"God has raised up Jim and Tammy Bakker as anointed ministers to reach the world with the Gospel. I've seen Jim and Tammy hold up through the years under incredible pressure. Their sustaining drive is their love for souls."

DR. CHARLES H. COOKMAN, North Carolina District Superintendent, Assemblies of God, Dunn, North Carolina

"It is an honor to include Heritage Village Church in our family of churches across the state of North Carolina. We are co-workers with the people who make up the congregation of Heritage Village Church in the quest to reach our world with the Gospel of Jesus Christ."

AIMEE GARCIA CORTESE, Prison Chaplain, Pastor, Crossroads Tabernacle, Bronx, New York

"Two vital elements in all of Jim and Tammy's work to reach the world for Christ are *faith* and *people*. Heritage USA is a place for people. In fact, I meet many who have visited the campground and retreat and say to me, 'I've never felt so much love.' That love is building faith in the hearts of people all over the world."

E RNEST U. FRANZONE, Senior Vice-President, Americana Hotels, Bedford, Texas

"Jim Bakker and the PTL ministry have given Christians at any economic level an opportunity to come to a special, worshipful environment that is the finest. They can worship together, enjoy and share their testimonies, and relax with their families. What an incredible blessing God has brought forth through Jim and Tammy!"

R EV. J. DON GEORGE, Pastor, Calvary Temple, Irving, Texas

"I have found that the PTL ministry greatly helps the work of building up local churches everywhere. Jim Bakker's ministry is so positive! It is amazing to see the effect Christian television is having by reaching into homes of every economic, political and social level."

D R. EVELYN CARTER SPENCER, Bible Teacher, Co-Pastor, House of Truth Church, Oakland, California

"I am excited, knowing that PTL will continue to grow dramatically because Jim Bakker and those who minister with him are committed to meeting the needs of people all over the world."

The Bakker family at home: Tammy Faye, Jim, Tammy Sue and Jamie Charles.

Then make me truly happy by loving
each other and agreeing wholeheartedly
with each other, working together with
one heart and mind and purpose.

PHILIPPIANS 2:2 TLB

Reverend Dortch and family at home.

I*f any man speak, let him speak as the oracles of God; if any man minister, let him do it as of the ability which God giveth; that God in all things may be glorified through Jesus Christ...*

I PETER 4:11 KJV

Supporting Pastor Bakker in meeting the many pressing, diverse needs of a growing congregation is a large staff of experienced, trained and compassionate pastors. These men and women offer individual counseling, make home and hospital visitations, teach seminars, devotionals and Sunday School classes, lead in worship and intercessory prayer, serve communion, participate in baptisms, weddings and funerals, and assist in all the other services of Christian ministry.

The pastors of Heritage Village Church at home and involved in their ministerial duties.

The pastors assist in weekly baptismal services at the Heritage Grand Ministry Center.

And the things that thou hast
heard of me among many
witnesses, the same commit
thou to faithful men,
who shall be able to teach
others also.

II TIMOTHY 2:2 KJV

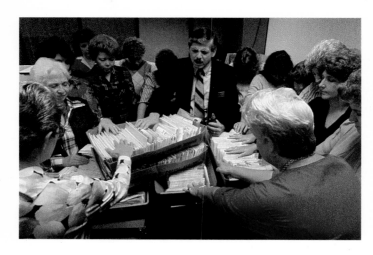

Pastors anoint prayer requests **(top left)** *and pray over the children* **(top right).** *Communion in the Upper Room* **(above)** *and personal counseling* **(right)** *are offered daily by the pastoral staff.*

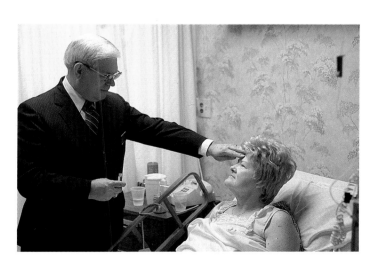

Anointing the sick, marrying, ministering to the ailing in hospitals and visiting campsites on horseback are all part of the duties of the team of ordained ministers at the Heritage Village Church.

HALL OF AGREEMENT

HAMILTON HUBBARD
DOROTHY HANNON
MARY STAER
MYRNA ELLIS
HOWARD HISBARD
ANN ROWLEY
GERALDINE ROWLEY
DONALD ROWLEY
MR. & MRS. PAUL DELEMBO
DANNY DELEMBO
DONALD J. GALBRAITH
EARLENE & VERNON LINDER
BARRY L. SIMPSON
MANUEL J. DELFINO
MRS. WILLIAM KESTER
BETTY CATES
FREDA BAKER
EDNA M. GRIM
CLAY & NORMA CRYER
JULIE R. JANDA
CLARENCE W. JOHNSON
MR. & MRS. JOHN J. HILL
BETTY GRIFFITH
JO ANN E. STURGEON & FAMILY
GEORGE & NADINE CLARK
LAWRENCE & JEANNIE BELLOWS
KRISTINE I. & STEPHEN H. KOELZ
DIANE SCHLAFER'S
EMMA PARK O'CONNOR
MRS. DON MISH
MARIE N. WALISAINEN
FRANK, MARLENE & ERIC GILNACK
MARIE LORD
BEVERLY B. FUNK
MRS. LOTTIE M. DIEHL
PRISCILLA DAHL-GILLOGLEY
EVA BRAUER
GARY & ANITA LORTON & FAMILY
NADINE DULL
DAVID WESTLAKE
MRS. GRADY HARRIS
ANN WESTFALL
WANDA J. MARSHALL
MR. & MRS. ROBERT MAYNARD
EUNICE W. KIRBY
LUCILLE & WESLEY SORN
MRS. DELTCIA A. HARTWELL
ART & GLORIA ROBLES
JUSTIN LEE BENDER
RICK & JAN STORY
MR. & MRS. WILLIAM A. THESLING
DR. E. G. SHERRELL
GIGI SHERRELL
JAN SHERRELL-GEPHARDT
PHYLLIS KLASSEN
SIR & MRS. WILLIAM LEE & FAMILY
KENNY STEGMAN
MARGARET B. TAYLOR
JOSEPH & BARBARA BESSIX
THOMAS & ETHEL HUGGINS
ANNA M. FLICKINGER
BILL & PAM GIBSON
JENNY BRITION
THE BERT LANCE FAMILY
NANCY & PETE JOHNSON
DOROTHY J. STARKWEATHER
BOB & JUANITA WALLIS
PAUL N. CHITWOOD
ALICE CHRISTINA RIKOS
DOROTHY M. NAVY
MALCOLM R. CROCKETT
JAMES C. ROARK
MR. & MRS. ...
MARY J. ...
MARY E. ...
FRANK ...
GREGORY ...

EDITH SLUSHER
MRS. J.B. GAMBRELL
MR. & MRS. FRANK E. TODD
ERDMAN PETZ
LEONARD & EDNA CATES
WAYNE GORDON WHITE
JAVAN FORT & FAMILY
ALICE L. SMITH
ELEANOR INGALLS
JAMES & MARY JO TAYLOR
MARK EDWARD LYNCH
JOHN MARK LYNCH
VIRGINIA GUNTER
REYNOLD WARNER
JERIMIAH GRIFFON & FAMILY
ROBERT MIGLICCIO & FAMILY
EDYTHE JONES
LOUISE & ROGER COOLEY
RICHARD BOWERS
CHAMEL & CAREY CONRAD
MR. & MRS. THOMAS ABEL
MR. & MRS. MARK BARKER
RUTH M. HOCH
MRS. WILLIAM SHUTE
FRED YATES, JR.
EMILY C. MICKA
MARWOOD C. HUGHES
ARLENE HUGHES
MARSHA EKAS
MR. & MRS. RALPH PARR
HENRY & NANCY KAMAY
TRUMAN CARROLL
B.J. METZGAR
MABEL YOKUM
MARGARITA DeLEON
TRINIDAD DeLEON
MS. H. KATHLEEN MICHAEL
CRAIG SHOLLENBERGER
JOYCE ROGERS
MARY K. ROSS
MR. & MRS. GLENN W. JENSON
HAZEL NANCE
SHIRLEY COX
RANDY CHARLES
MR. & MRS. MADDING
MARY A. MALCOLM
ROSE GERZENY-ROBAK
VIRGIL GROSSMAN
MR. & MRS. JOHN E. VAN EPPS
MR. & MRS. GERALD F. LENTZ
JOE & MILDRED LYONS
AUGUST NICKEL FAMILY
MR. & MRS. JOHN A. HUNTER
CARL & VIVIAN BUCKNER
CHARLES & RITA VANCE
LEE & DOROTHY McCORD
BARBARA J. HOWELL
JOHN SUMMERFIELD
MR. & MRS. FRANK ERNST
MRS. EULA JONES
ERVIN & LUCILLE RINSCH
THE MONTOTO EQUINO FAMILY
SUZANNE GILLELAND
ARTHUR W. OTTERBEIN
JESSIE S. OTTERBEIN
JOHN R. O...

HAROLD & EDITH MINNER
BOBBY & JANICE WOOD & FAMILY
LAWRENCE & CANDY GARCIA
JAMES MASTERSON
HARRY SMITH, SR. & FAMILY
OWEN & BETTY HEATH
JULIE RORISON
I. RENE KAYORIE
DYAN BONTER
JERRY & LILLIAN OLLINGER
MR. & MRS. BERNIE CASH
MORTON FAMILY
MRS. JOYCE FOSTER
YVONNE FURTADO
DAWNA & HEATHER WYLLIE
DENISE CHOINIERE
ELDON & ROSALIE McFARLAND
SID & BETTY YOUNG
MRS. MARGARET BOGIE
EM & ESTELLA CLARK
MIRA HALVORSEN
WALTER HALVORSEN
ADA GEHRING
FLORENCE SHCIEICHER
WILLIAM P. MAVITY
ALFERIA NICOLE BAILEY
RICHARD & DIANE ELLENZBURG
ARLYN & JARED HART-MESSER
EVELYN ROUTH
ANNIE D. CABE
TONY LORTIE
ROBERT ORRIS & CHARLES ROBAK
FUNMILAYO SOYEMI ODENIYI
JOHN & FRANCES ZAJACK
MRS. EMILY CAMPBELL
CATHERINE AMES
REV. LOUIS W. ACREE
TOMMY HARRIS, SR.
SALLIE J. HARRIS
GEORGE E. HARRIS
TOMMY HARRIS, JR.
MR. & MRS. GEORGE E. BELTZ
CLAIRE A. KING
SANDRA L. YATES & MOTHER
BARBARA JO TIMKO
DAVID & JENNI WEBER & CHILDREN
BOB & ELLEN GUST & FAMILY
FREDDIE, WILMA & KEVIN COOPER
FRED LUEDTKE FAMILY
JANE GOODE
LARRY & MELINDA DeFORE
DORIS & OTTO PLATT
STEVE & LANITA EWERS
ARTHUR LEE THOMASSON, III
WILLIAM A. THOMASSON
GEORGE ANDERSON
NELDA PALMER
SCOTT HENDRICKS
ELENA M. AMOR
DAVID H. & VICKI McCLESKEY
MR. & MRS. M.L. REEVES
RICHARD FLANERY
DAVID BONNELL
RALPH PEREZ MONTOTO
JAMES & LEAH SPEAKS
RON DYE
NELL CLOUDY FAMILY
CLARENCE & GEORGIA WARNER
PATRICA ANN WILLE
THE HETTINGA FAMILY
ROBERT, ADA & DOROTHY REDICK
BILL & DIANE GERBER BAUGH
WRAY & DOROTHY STAUB
ROY W. HOSIER, JR.
...EY & MRS. CHARLES W. JOHNSTON
...TH ALLEN FUETTER
...RTHUR & FLORENCE KALLIN
...SIAH ELLIOTT
...RY & ANN SONDLES
... HAZEL PEREIRA
...LOS & DORIS MILON
...IE WALLACE
... WALLACE
... HALL
...ARY DeLUCA
...OTT
...L. LEE
...TE DINGELACKER
...BARBARA WOOD
...RTT REAL ESTATE
...GUS
...DONNA HULEHAN
...WILLIAM REDEN
...RTHUR BONKOWSKI

PAT & LARRY FRISBU
JANICE HALL
MARIE ELIZABETH LEDOUX
GREG EDWARD SILVA
VEE VAN DER VOORT
MR. & MRS. FRED E. BALL
MR. & MRS. J.B. HARRELL
RON & JOAN ASHTON
MARY ALICE SHANNON
MRS. STELLA RESIM
JIM TARBET
EMMA SHAW
DENNY LAUDENSLAGER
DAVID & JENETTA McCAIN
MARY TOMMASONE
PHYLLIS LUEL
MR. & MRS. ROSS L. WAGAR
BARBARA VAN BUREN
REV. & MRS. H.D. HOBBS
GARY V. ATKINS
LOUISE POTTER
THE DOV
DONALD RAEF & FAMILY
EDWARD YOUNG, JR.
PAUL & ESTHER MILLER
B.K. FREEMAN
JESSIE & VIRGINIA HODGES
MR. & MRS. RUSSELL POTTS
HYLAND & FLORA RAMBO & FAMILY
ALBERTA JEFFRIES
GREGORY B. TRISCOTT
DAN DOYLE
ANNA DeVAUGHN
JIMMIE BOGGS
SARAH ANN DAVIS & CHILDREN
KATHERINE & CHARLES SPEAKMAN
LUCILLE H. EVANS
JACK O. WATSON
TAD MASTERSON
JONATHAN RODGERS
LINDA FODE
ORVAL SWANSON
MARY BESICH
MILDRED STRANG
DIANNE STELLMEIER
JULEA W. HAMMOND
EVELYN SISLER
CAMILLE HALL
TOM & DOROTHY MOSLEY
CAROLYN & HATTIE OVERTON
MR. & MRS. WALTON C. ASHLEY, SR.
REED M. ASHLEY & FAMILY
WALTON C. ASHLEY, JR. & FAMILY
JANET E. HENSON & FAMILY
MRS. KATHERINE HENDERSON
LUCINDA NEWELL
DE WYNA GANT
TABITHA & CASSANDRA MURPHY
BETTY RHODES
JEWELL CUTHBERTSON
R.A. HEROLD
BRIAN D. CARROLL
MR. & MRS. N.A. DENTON
RANDY SNELGROVE
CYNTHIA JOHNSON
TEOFILO BRYAN
JOSEPHINE GUASH
DREMA L. MORRIS
RUTH GRESHAM
GLEN YORK
DAN TROMP
RUSS & MARY E. YOST
MR. & MRS. DAVID E. HAMILTON
MARY COLLIS
CAROL M. GREEN
MRS. WESLEY NELSON
LENTA PENNY
JOSEPH A. STASY
DURHAM JOHNSON
GLADYS L. CRAFT
BARBARA M...
MIKE & EVA...

HELEN KIMBLE
MRS. NELLIE E. PEER
DENNA J. BENNETT
ROBERT STETTLER
DOROTHY POPEJOY
ADA CROUSE
ULYSSES GILLETTE
CHUCK & DUGAN DIKES
MAURICE T. SNYDER
KRISTI SNYDER
MELVIN E. SNYDER
MATTHEW DAVID DIKES
SHARON J. TIMMONS
RICHARD & JANICE NIBSCHLER
LAWN & GAIL BASE
VIOLA KENNEDY
GARRY & BETTY OSBORNE
MR. & MRS. LYNN KUHN
JOHN & MARY BELL
MR. & MRS. WILLIAM R. BOLING, JR.
JOHANNES G. JAKAT
ALBERT JOHN REHM, III
ALLEGRA M. WALDEN
MR. & MRS. EDGAR BRAME
LOLA M. EATON
MYRTLE HUNNEL
STAN A. VARNA HARE
FRED & FREDA PARMESANG
HILLARY LYNN SNYDER
LINDA ROGERS
JOE & PAM NARBAIT
DANIEL & JEANETTE NARBAIT
DON RUSS
ALICE JOHNSON
ELSIE HEYWOOD
WALTER HEYWOOD
MARY & ANDY SENZAK
WILLIAM REISHER
SHIRLEY REISHER
TIM REISHER
TIM MICKEY
TONYA MICKEY
JEREMY MICKEY
JARON MICKEY
NICHOLE MICKEY
MRS. IRENE CLOCK
VICTOR CLOCK
NORMAN CLOCK
PHILIP CLOCK
JAMES CLOCK
DAVID P. SCHULTZ
DEBORAH A. SCHULTZ
ERIC HOTOPP
CHRISTOPHER T. HOTOPP
SARAH E. SCHULTZ
ROBERT C. COOPER
FORREST & ALENE ROBERTSON
YOLANDA SI SOTO
MARION A. PURVIANCE
ARLENE RICE
J.T. CRAVEN
W.A. & BARBARA LAGLEY
DOROTHY E. SPRINHOUR
MR. & MRS. THOMAS POWELL, SR.
WILLIE MEEAN
MARY & LOUIE HARTWICK
MRS. DOLORES R. SMITH
WILMA E. HAWKINS
JIMMY & SHIRLEY FRAZIER

Pray for each other so that you may be healed. The earnest prayer of a righteous man has great power and wonderful results.

JAMES 5:16 TLB

*Thousands of prayer partners' names are displayed in the Hall of Agreement **(opposite and right)**. Phone counselors **(below)** assist callers and a church member **(below right)** opens his home for prayer and fellowship.*

Prayer is the foundation upon which the Heritage Village Church is built. The Church believes in and practices constant prayer for the needs of its people, the nation and the world. There is no burden so great, no need so insignificant, no situation so grave as to be beyond the power of prayer.

*When you meet together some will sing,
another will teach...but everything that is
done must be useful to all, and build them
up in the Lord.*

I CORINTHIANS 14:26 TLB

Sunday morning worship service is not complete without the ministry of the Heritage Village Church Choir. Through beautiful renderings of traditional and contemporary hymns, the choir voices the hope, the love, and the life-changing power of Jesus Christ.

*Sunday morning praise (**opposite**) at the Heritage Village Church. The church choir (**below**) presents "The Living Cross" during the Easter season.*

Phone counselors respond to partners' calls during a telethon.

B*ring all the tithes into the storehouse so that there will be food enough in my Temple...*

MALACHI 3:10 TLB

Giving is a faithful element of worship at Heritage Village Church. From the beginning, the PTL family, at home and around the world, has rallied behind the church's mission to carry the Gospel "unto the uttermost part of the earth." Their prayerful financial support has enabled Pastor Bakker to follow God's calling.

Support comes in many different ways—tithes and daily offerings, faithful partner-giving through the mail, the church bookstore and giftshop, retreat-lodging fees, gifts and bequests, and special fund-raising events.

The integrity in stewardship of Heritage Village Church is exemplified by PTL's charter membership in the ECFA (Evangelical Council of Financial Accountability) and is confirmed by the internationally respected auditors Deloitte Haskins and Sells, and Laventhol and Horwath.

One of the charity auctions (top) which raised donations to help build Fort Hope and (left) answering calls during the church's telethon. The church bookstore in the Ministry Center (right) provides Christian literature for all ages.

And whoso shall receive one such little child in my name receiveth me.

MATTHEW 18:5 KJV

*Tender loving care **(top)** in the church day care facility. Instruction is provided for children of all ages **(above)** during the Sunday morning worship service.*

Young children are offered an atmosphere of love, cheerful recreation, and specialized Bible and educational instruction at the Heritage Village Church day-care facility.

This fully-certified service is available to church members and visitors alike, and is dedicated to meeting the total needs of the preschoolers in its care. Within this secure Christian environment, the children develop physically, emotionally and socially.

*Train up a child in the way
he should go: and when he is old,
he will not depart from it.*

PROVERBS 22:6 KJV

Pastors Jim and Tammy Bakker believe that instruction in God's Word is essential to Christian growth for people of all ages. The Heritage Village Church Sunday School Department provides weekly classes led by a staff of trained teachers. Supplementing these classes are special teaching programs for young children and teenagers and electives for adults.

Royal Rangers and Missionettes (right and below) enjoy studying the adventure of God's Word.

Heritage Village Church Academy offers standards of academic excellence, spiritual growth and total character-development to students from kindergarten through twelfth grade. Dedicated teachers make learning enjoyable for students, encouraging them in making right choices for the future.

With individualized education, the Academy provides training for students to pursue careers in the professions, the fine arts, and the trades, all within the context of strong Christian citizenship.

*Class in session **(above left)** at Heritage Academy and **(above right)** Jamie Charles Bakker. Academy students **(below)** combine lunch time with learning.*

54

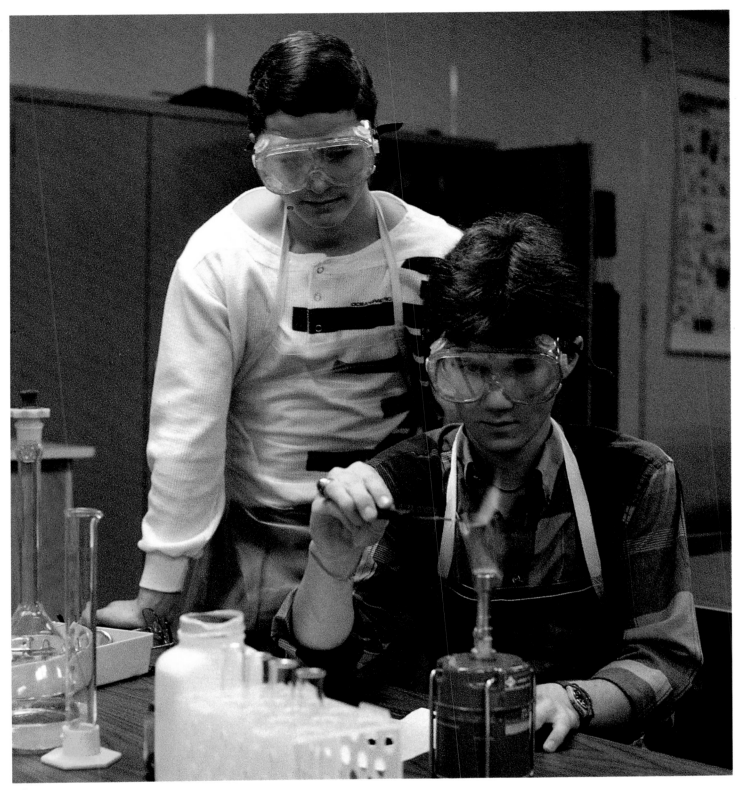

Chemistry lab at the Heritage Academy.

Study to shew thyself approved unto God, a
workman that needeth not to be ashamed,
rightly dividing the word of truth.

II TIMOTHY 2:15 KJV

 D on't let anyone think little of you because you are young. Be their ideal; let them follow the way you teach and live; be a pattern for them in your love, your faith, and your clean thoughts.

I TIMOTHY 4:12 TLB

The Family Center serves as a hub for Heritage Village Church youth. Basketball **(top left)** for boys and girls teaches teamwork, and roller skating **(below)** offers great fun and good exercise.

Heritage USA provides opportunities for young people to come together in fellowship and enjoy wholesome fun and recreation with Christ as the center of every activity.

The Heritage Village Church youth program helps today's young people grow in their relationships with the Lord Jesus Christ, with their families and with their peers.

Here they have special activities including church services, Christian concerts, teaching seminars, retreats, sports competitions, television programming and a youth magazine. The young—and those they touch—are being trained and equipped for Christian leadership in the 21st Century.

*Young people find a full range of wholesome activities at Heritage USA, eating pizza **(top right)** and roller skating at the Family Center **(above)**, or worshipping together during a musical presentation. "The most important people in Heritage Village Church are our youth. They are the church of tomorrow."*
—*Jim Bakker*

Heritage USA, a place of recreation and fellowship.

M*ay you always be doing those good, kind things which show that you are a child of God, for this will bring much praise and glory to the Lord.*

PHILIPPIANS 1:11 TLB

Realizing the significant role of the single adult, the church has developed vital programs designed to meet the unique needs of the widowed, the unmarried, the single parent and the divorced. In a loving and caring community, Heritage Village Church offers encouragement and fellowship, through national singles conferences, banquets, classes and retreats.

Love each other with brotherly affection and take delight in honoring each other. Never be lazy in your work but serve the Lord enthusiastically.

ROMANS 12:10-11 TLB

Heritage Village Church is building Christian leaders for today and tomorrow through its outreaches of Men's Fellowship and Women's Ministries.

Whether ministering in the prisons, camping out with the Royal Rangers, or repairing a roof for an elderly couple, the Men's Fellowship takes an active role in meeting the needs of the church community.

Serving the women at the Heritage House, visiting the sick in the hospitals, and fixing meals for shut-ins are just a few of the diverse activities of the Women's Ministries. In addition, they provide programs that help women realize their full potential in Christ.

Responding to the desperate need for a shelter for street people, the men of Heritage Village Church labor tirelessly to complete Fort Hope.

You shall give due honor and respect to the elderly, in the fear of God.

LEVITICUS 19:32 TLB

"I remember the day," says Jim Bakker, "when they told my Grandma Irwin she was too old to teach her class. She was forced to 'retire' from Sunday school. That was like a death sentence to my Grandma—she had so much to offer! I am building a place where the elderly and retired can come and feel loved and wanted...a place where they can *refire* instead of retire. This is a community where the elderly can contribute their wisdom and experience and enjoy some of the most productive years of their lives."

Heritage USA is a place where many retired people come to share their extensive talents, and to be "refired" in Christian service. Lovely houses, condominiums, and efficiency apartments currently provide quality homes in a surrounding of fellowship and daily Christian activity within the Church.

Warm fellowship, lovely housing, and the closeness and security of a Christian community make Heritage USA an ideal home for senior citizens.

The community of Heritage USA is designed to make the elderly feel loved and needed. Here, they can contribute their wisdom and experience and enjoy some of their most productive years.

(**right**) *Pastor Richard Dortch and Uncle Henry Harrison minister to their friend.*

Work hard and cheerfully at all you do, just as though you were working for the Lord and not merely for your masters, remembering that it is the Lord Christ who is going to pay you, giving you your full portion of all he owns. He is the one you are really working for.

COLOSSIANS 3:23-24 TLB

A doctor, an attorney, a commercial pilot and a veterinarian—these are among the 1,000 volunteers who contribute an average of 22,000 hours every month in virtually every part of the work of Heritage Village Church.

Since the beginning, volunteers have played a vital role in helping the Christian Church fulfill its mission to reach the world with the message of Christ. The same is true today at Heritage Village Church. Volunteers offer their time, their talents and their resources as school teachers, ushers, drivers, carpenters, receptionists, and phone counselors, serving wherever and whenever they are needed.

Contributing whatever time they can, all volunteers see this work as their ministry for the Lord; some have even moved to Heritage USA with the express purpose of volunteering. These committed men and women presently comprise one of the largest, most outstanding volunteer forces of its kind in the nation.

One of the church's dedicated volunteers **(opposite)** *works in the distribution center. For both the young and the retired* **(below)** *, volunteering is their greatest contribution to the church, and one of their greatest sources of satisfaction.*

These all continued with one accord in prayer and supplication...

ACTS 1:14 KJV

The Upper Room is the spiritual focal point of Heritage Village Church...a sanctuary where prayers are offered up throughout the day and night.

God promised that this would be a place of divine appointment, where He would fulfill the expectancy of those who enter, along with the millions who send their requests and photos to the Upper Room for prayer.

On the night of its dedication, Pastor Bakker declared, "In these last days, the Upper Room will be a place where united prayer will ascend to God twenty-four hours a day on behalf of His people so that we too may be empowered to live triumphant, overcoming lives, and to preach the Gospel to the ends of the earth."

Evening communion in the Upper Room.

Fundamental to all that Heritage Village Church does on a worldwide scale is the witness of what it does next to its own door, fulfilling Christ's mandate to ''...preach the gospel to the poor...to heal the brokenhearted, to preach deliverance to the captives, and recovering of sight to the blind, to set at liberty them that are bruised'' (Luke 4:18 KJV).

Each day, the compassionate hand of Heritage Village Church reaches out through its grass-roots ministries, rescuing those who would otherwise perish without the saving hand of Jesus Christ.

Weekly auctions at the Heritage Village Auction Barn help support local home missions. Proceeds from items—many of which are donated—help to underwrite the expenses of Fort Hope, Heritage House and the People That Love Center.

PTL prison workers offer literature, food and spiritual encouragement to prisoners.

Remember those in prison as if you were their fellow prisoners...

HEBREWS 13:3 NIV

Heritage Village Church has faithfully obeyed the Lord's command to visit those in prison, and has established one of the most extensive prison ministries in the world. A ministry staff and network of over 8,000 volunteer workers reaches into more than 1,000 jails and prisons in America and 14 foreign countries.

As a result of Heritage Village Church's donation and installation of satellite receiving systems, prisoners in high-security correctional facilities receive 24 hours of daily Christian programming through PTL. For many, this is their only source of encouragement and hope. Each year, PTL distributes more than 25,000 Bibles to prisoners, gives out over a quarter-of-a-million pieces of Christian literature, and communicates with thousands of inmates who study the Bible through correspondence courses.

The vital follow-up ministry of the church includes visiting prisoners' families, helping prisoners find employment, fellowship, encouragement, housing, and providing after-care ministry upon their release from prison.

Heritage Village Church is a leader in the Coalition of Prison Evangelists and a sponsor of the 1986 National Simultaneous Prison Revival. The ministry also sponsors national, regional, and state prison ministry conferences, which effectively train prison workers and chaplains.

"I have been in prison for 5 years. Until 18 months ago, I did not know the Lord. Because of very little schooling, I couldn't read the Bible.

"Then PTL television came to our prison with programs 5 days a week and Sunday evenings. Through PTL, I came to know the Lord.

"A year ago, you sent me the New Testament on tape. What a blessing as I listen to the tapes and follow along in my Bible."   —Paul E.

Jim Bakker (left) poses in front of newly installed satellite dish at Huttonsville Correctional Center in Huttonsville, West Virginia. Dedication service (above) for the Huttonsville satellite dish.

*For I was an hungered, and ye gave me meat: I was
thirsty, and ye gave me drink: I was a stranger, and
ye took me in: naked, and ye clothed me: I was sick,
and ye visited me: I was in prison, and ye came
unto me...Inasmuch as ye have done it unto
one of the least of these my brethren,
ye have done it unto me.*

MATTHEW 25:35,36,40 KJV

*Volunteer distributes groceries **(above)** at People That Love Center. The flagship People That Love
Center in Fort Mill, South Carolina **(top right).** Clothing, in addition to food **(bottom right),** is
available to the needy.*

President Reagan declared, "The PTL Television Network is carrying out a master plan for 'People That Love,' opening centers all across the country to provide food, clothing, furniture, and job-bank centers at no cost."

The compassionate caring nature of Heritage Village Church is also demonstrated through the nationwide network of nearly 1,000 People That Love Centers. These Centers in every state and in twelve foreign countries are providing emergency foods, clothing, furniture and household items, as well as spiritual counsel, prayer, employment assistance, financial advice, and community service referrals. Through this outreach, the church responds to the needs of 10 million people each year, rebuilding lives and restoring dignity.

Pastor Bakker and President Reagan.

*And the gospel must first be published
among all nations.*

MARK 13:10 KJV

Afirm belief in the lasting power of the printed page and a need for top quality audio and visual recordings caused Pastors Jim and Tammy Bakker to establish Heritage Village Church Publications, which distributes millions of Bibles, books, tapes and records.

This publishing arm of the church produces invaluable ministry aids which are distributed internationally on a regular basis. Ongoing publications include church and partner-oriented literature, devotional and teaching books, and periodicals for the prison ministry.

Over and above all this stands the work of Heritage Village Church in printing, publishing, and distributing Holy Scriptures. For example, Heritage Village Church is producing Bibles which will be distributed free of charge inside the People's Republic of China. In these ways the ministry of Pastor Bakker and Heritage Village Church takes its place among the great societies whose work in the dissemination of the Gospel has played a vital part in the salvation of the world.

If a brother or sister be naked, and destitute of daily food, and one of you say unto them, Depart in peace, be ye warmed and filled; notwithstanding ye give them not those things which are needful to the body; what doth it profit?

JAMES 2:15,16 KJV

Responding to a desperate need on the part of America's homeless, Heritage Village Church established a missionary outreach to house and restore those "forgotten" people.

Fort Hope is designed to help America's "street people" begin new lives through counseling, educational and vocational training, and sound, biblical teaching. In a secure family-like atmosphere, trained staff members and volunteers lovingly nurture and help rebuild these brothers and sisters who have had broken lives, so that they may again become productive members of our society.

"Through the ministry of PTL, I came to Christ in jail, but when I got out I had no money or a place to go, so Fort Hope took me. Now I'm growing in Christ, working and discovering God's blessings daily." —Keith D.

"I was a cocaine junkie for 6 years. It destroyed my respect for everyone, especially myself. I came here with nothing, only wanting to get off drugs. Through prayer, I've been delivered and have come to a new awakening of God's love and power.

"God has shown me so much love through the staff and the other men. I am full of joy over what God has done for me." —Ron M.

Residents of Fort Hope in a Bible study class.

Renewing commitments and receiving spiritual support at a New Vine Fellowship meeting.

Now unto him that is able to do exceeding
abundantly above all that we ask or think,
according to the power that worketh in us.

EPHESIANS 3:20 KJV

The church's responsibility includes responding to the needs of men, women and families whose lives have been shattered by alcohol and drugs. Through its New Vine Fellowship, Heritage Village Church provides a loving, spiritual and non-judgmental atmosphere for those who are battling and overcoming alcoholism and drug addiction. Together, they share their struggles, receive counseling and encouragement, and discover their source of strength, deliverance and new life in Jesus Christ. There are now more than 70 New Vine Fellowships throughout the nation, cooperating with an expanding network of over 300 ministries. Those who have triumphed and are living lives free of alcohol and drugs regularly speak before youth and community groups to educate and help to stem the ravages of drug and alcohol abuse.

> As we have therefore opportunity, let us do
> good unto all men, especially unto them who
> are of the household of faith.
>
> GALATIANS 6:10 KJV

Pastor Jim Bakker and the Heritage Village Church are committed to sharing God's love in tangible, practical ways and have given millions of dollars to organizations that are helping meet a variety of human needs.

Over the years, the church has extended its hand to help victims in emergency situations, support colleges and universities, to rebuild churches, to distribute food and literature to the underprivileged, and to provide matching funds to local churches in order to assist families in crisis situations.

Heritage Village Church donates regularly to United Way, March of Dimes, Muscular Dystrophy of America and Goodwill Industries. Other agencies supported by PTL include Food for the Hungry, Crisis Assistance, Empty Stocking Fund, National Inner-City Ministry, Parson of the Hills and the Salvation Army.

Heritage Village Church rebuilt Bethel AME Zion Church in 1976 after it was destroyed by fire.

The church also regularly supports Boys Town and Goodwill Industries.

*You made all the delicate, inner parts of my body,
and knit them together in my mother's womb…
You saw me before I was born and scheduled each day
of my life before I began to breathe.*

PSALM 139:13,16 TLB

The 1973 decision to legalize abortion has resulted in the shameless murder of the unborn at the appalling rate of 1.5 million babies a year. Heritage Village Church took a strong, biblical stand against abortion, but soon realized that this protest was not enough.

Rather than simply condemn this evil, Heritage Village Church opened the beautiful Heritage House in July, 1984 for those expectant mothers who have chosen birth rather than abortion. In the secure environment of the Heritage House, women receive spiritual guidance and education, while completing their pregnancies. In a loving, family setting, the women learn and share the responsibilities of cooking, pre-natal care and proper nutrition, and have the opportunity to receive further education, part-time employment and professional counseling. Heritage House, a fully-licensed facility and a founding member of the American Coalition of Alternatives to Abortion, has helped to establish a network of over 40 Christian maternity homes.

As an extension of the Heritage House ministry, the church's 24-hour hotline has been able to respond to the needs of thousands of women in critical pregnancy situations.

Heritage Village Church's "Tender Loving

The Heritage House provides a comfortable atmosphere for fellowship and learning.

76

Courtyard of Heritage House.

Care" Adoption Agency is fully accredited and helps each expectant mother determine the best choices for herself and her baby. The families in the church assist the agency by providing foster care for newborn infants. During the first year of its existence many childless Christian couples experienced the wonderful joy of parenthood through the ministry of the Adoption Agency.

"Had it not been for Jim and Tammy Bakker and Heritage House, my baby would not be alive today...and neither would I.

"Now we both have a future. With God's help, we can make it. Thanks for taking a stand and reaching out with love." —Lisa

"For four years, we tried to have a baby.

After heartaches and disappointments, God began showing us a plan.

"We mailed our application to PTL's Tender Loving Care Adoption Agency and prayed, believing for a baby girl who we could dedicate on Christmas Sunday. Later, we learned that your adoption agency staff prays over each application and each baby, asking for God's perfect will.

"The prayers were answered and our miracle happened. As we bathe, feed, rock and watch our precious daughter grow each day, we rejoice in the greatness of our God.

"Jim and Tammy, I wish we could see you in person and give you both a big hug!"
—Proud Adoptive Parents.

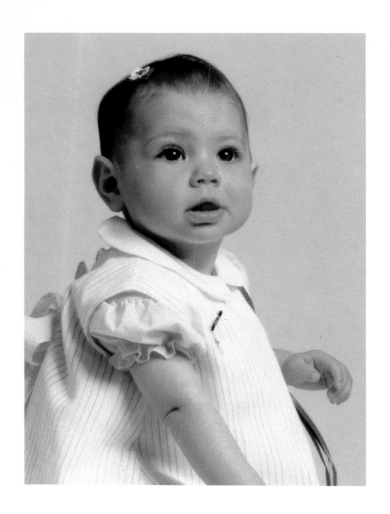

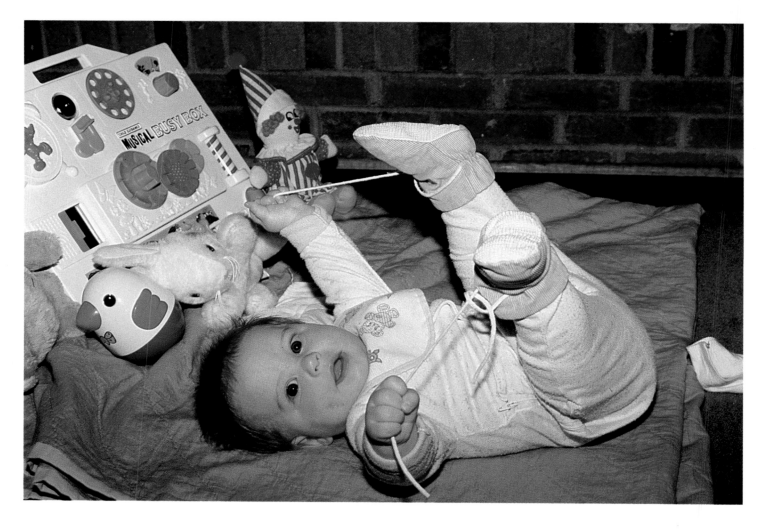

*Some of the precious lives **(below and opposite)** that have been saved through the outreach of the Heritage House. A church family **(above)** "adopts" an expectant mother during her stay.*

A compassionate staff of secretaries prayerfully reads and responds to each letter sent to the Heritage Village Church.

And these things write we unto you, that
your joy may be full.

I JOHN 1:4 KJV

At the heart of the church is a sensitive, personal response to the thousands of letters received daily. This critical one-on-one ministry through the mail is accomplished by a compassionate staff of personal secretaries who read and respond to the varied and vital needs expressed. Whether requesting spiritual guidance, ministry-related information or literature, every letter receives an answer. Requests are prayed for individually and then sent to the Upper Room for anointing. Urgent needs receive immediate attention by the Pastoral Follow-up Department; in critical, life-threatening situations, a local pastor is contacted and sent directly to the individual. More than 8,000 pastors in all 50 states cooperate with the Heritage Village Church in meeting these needs.

Whoso loveth instruction loveth knowledge...

PROVERBS 12:1, KJV

"My vision and mission for the school is to prepare a task force of dedicated men and women, trained in the latest evangelistic and modern media techniques, to reach our world for Jesus Christ." —Jim Bakker

In 1978 the Heritage Village Church opened the Heritage School of Evangelism and Communications, an ideal academic program that combines classroom instruction with practical training in various mission fields. Today, Heritage students are involved in specialized "hands-on" experience in television production, video and audio technology, counseling, evangelism, graphic arts and design, journalism and radio production. Of the hundreds of students who have graduated from the School of Evangelism and Communications, over 90 percent are involved in full-time ministry, utilizing their valuable training in churches and ministries throughout the United States and in twenty foreign countries.

Heritage School of Evangelism and Communications has a cooperative program with North Central Bible College in Minneapolis, Minnesota which allows students to receive college credit for internship training.

Heritage School of Evangelism students gain hands-on experience in various departments of the church.

A marriage workshop (opposite) at Heritage Village Church. A healed marriage (above) and a new life together.

*And all things are of God, who hath
reconciled us to himself by Jesus Christ, and
hath given to us the ministry of
reconciliation.*

II CORINTHIANS 5:18 KJV

The Workshop Ministry of Heritage Village Church was born out of Pastor Bakker's deep alarm at all the pressures that are destroying so many marriages and families today.

Here, within the sheltering, protective arms of the Body of Christ, men and women whose lives and marriages are threatened with destruction find forgiveness, new hope, and new love.

This revolutionary ministry combines the principles of God's Word with sound, psychological techniques to help bring emotional, mental and spiritual wholeness. The workshops are scheduled regularly throughout the year in the PTL Partner Center, and are led by a ministry team of professionally trained counselors.

Thousands of marriages—many on the brink of divorce—have been restored and revitalized through these highly successful marriage workshops. In the inner healing and personal growth workshops, thousands more have found complete healing of their emotions through the power of Jesus Christ.

Demand for the workshops continues to increase as word of the ministry's results spreads throughout the nations. Because of the concentrated demand in various geographic locations, PTL has held marriage workshops in Hawaii, California, and Toronto, Canada, where thousands of lives were transformed.

*G*o *ye into all the world, and preach the*
gospel to every creature.

MARK 16:15 KJV

Heritage Village Church fulfills Christ's mandate through an immense television outreach that penetrates 52 nations around the world with the Word of Jesus...a mission that would be impossible without the medium of television. PTL is sensitive to the diversity of cultures that it serves; knowing this variety to be a gift from God. Therefore *PTL does not impose.* Rather than simply 'dubbing' American English-speaking programs into other languages, Pastor Bakker's vision from the beginning was to create programs that could be hosted by local spiritual frontrunners, with a flavor and a format appealing to people through their own languages and cultures. This was a revolutionary concept in Christian television.

In January, 1977, PTL launched its first foreign production—the Spanish "Club PTL"—and has produced French, Italian, Japanese, Thai, African, Chinese and Filipino programs. Jim and Tammy Bakker are not featured on these programs—although the Heritage Village

Some of the church's foreign television hosts **(above)** *join Jim during a telethon and* **(above right)** *the Chinese PTL television broadcast.* **(right)** *Carrying a great burden for both Jews and Arabs, Pastor Bakker has intensified the church's efforts to reach the Middle East with the Gospel.*

"Entr' Amis," PTL's French Christian television program, being taped in the church's studios *(above)*. Pastor Bakker anoints a pastor for the ministry *(left)* while visiting with partners in Hawaii during his worldwide missions trip.

*The bustling streets of Hong Kong (top).
Gifts from the congregation and partners help
provide bread and milk for children in Cal-
cutta (above) and donations helped build the
Kaokapukur Assemblies of God Bible School
in India (right).*

Church has been underwriting nearly all production costs until the programs become self-supporting and independent.

This massive international outreach is helping lead souls around the world to the Savior and is actually building local Christian churches. The PTL programs have helped to spark nationwide revivals in many countries.

In some places, such as Zimbabwe and Thailand, PTL has been the only television program permitted to openly declare God's Word. Heritage Village Church also responds to worldwide needs in many other ways. Working hand in hand with missionary organizations around the globe, Heritage Village Church has helped to build schools and hospitals, feed and clothe the hungry, offer shelter to those displaced by war and famine, and train men and women to present the Gospel to those of their own cultures.

*Dr. Paul Yonggi Cho (**above left**) visits with church leaders at the Heritage Village Church. Pastor Bakker (**above**) dedicates an infant in a Nigerian church during his worldwide mission trip. (**left**) The PTL office in Panama.*

An old-fashioned camp meeting.

N*ot forsaking the assembling of ourselves together, as the manner of some is; but exhorting one another: and so much the more, as ye see the day approaching.*

HEBREWS 10:25 KJV

From the early decades of the 19th Century right up through the years of the Great Depression a stirring chapter in American history unfolded with the growth of the great camp meetings. Multitudes gathered at brush arbors and campgrounds across the country to hear legendary revivalists—Methodists, Baptists and Pentecostals.

During boyhood summers in Michigan, Jim Bakker attended camp where he had his most moving spiritual experiences in an old tabernacle with a sawdust floor. Even then, looking beyond the stuffy cabins with lumpy mattresses, looking beyond the muddy swimming holes and "outdoor plumbing" he dreamed of a day when God's people could come together in beautiful, pleasant surroundings.

A "modern" Christian campground during the 1940's.

IN THE GROVE, MARANATHA PARK, GREEN LANE, PA.

*Our country's pioneer Christian campgrounds offered the "latest" in restaurants and lodging accommodations (**above and opposite**).*

Aware that lifestyle was changing in 20th-Century America, Jim knew that drab, outmoded campgrounds would no longer appeal to Christians who were taking their vacations in clean, modern, well-planned but secular theme parks and recreation centers. God impressed on Jim and the Heritage Village Church the need to carry the spirit of the campmeeting movement into the 21st Century, and the concept of Heritage USA came into being. From the beginning, Pastor Bakker envisioned an exciting, total-living community where the diverse needs of Christians could be met, both old and young together.

South Carolina (above): a place of breathtaking beauty. (left) Pastor Bakker reviews plans for the Main Auditorium of the church.

God had already chosen the location— more than four square miles astride the border of North and South Carolina, a site miraculously preserved from the surrounding urban and commercial development. On January 2, 1978, ground was broken. The name "Heritage USA" expressed a commitment to preserve our Christian and American heritage.

Fort Heritage Campground, which opened in the summer of 1978, featured hundreds of campsites, fully equipped with water, electricity, cable-TV hookups, picnic tables, charcoal grills and convenient, modern bath facilities. Rustic yet thoroughly modern chalets were constructed, a 3,500-seat outdoor amphitheater was carved out of the Carolina clay, and work began on the building of a comprehensive recreation village. A highly publicized "log-cutting" ceremony was celebrated on July 4th of that year, and thousands of campers jammed into the grounds to participate.

*Log cutting ceremony **(above left)** at the dedication of Heritage USA. The campgrounds at Heritage USA **(above right and below)** provide delight for all ages.*

Campers and residents find a varied selection of food and supplies at the General Store **(top)** and receive emergency medical treatment at the Heritage USA Medical Center **(above)**. Recreation Village **(left)** includes an Olympic-size pool, restaurants and recreational facilities.

The congregation (above) entering the sanctuary of Heritage Village Church. (opposite top) Burning the Heritage USA mortgage note and (opposite below) worship during the dedication of the Main Auditorium on Victory Day, 1980.

God's ways are not our ways. A series of devastating blows halted further development for nearly eighteen months. But God's people rallied behind Pastor Bakker and on Labor Day, 1980, a great victory was celebrated for several days with the first "Victory Day" parade and the completion and dedication of the Main Auditorium of the Heritage Village Church.

"It's over—the battle has been won! A few months ago, the site was just a blatant reminder of defeat, and today, it's a glorious monument of victory to the God we serve."

—Jim Bakker, "Victory Day," 1980

Many battles remained. The ministry was separated among eight widely-scattered locations, but the church moved forward by completing the World Outreach Center in 1981, creating a new headquarters for the ministry. The struggle intensified, as a series of financial crises followed. Critics openly predicted the demise of the ministry. But as Pastor Bakker walked through the grounds, faced with the knowledge that his dream was on the point of being shattered, God spoke to him and told him to build an Upper Room of intercessory prayer.

"If you will build this for Me," said the Lord, "then I will save your ministry."

*The historic Upper Room **(above)** in Jerusalem. **(opposite)** The Upper Room at Heritage USA.*

There followed a fact-finding mission to the historic Upper Room in Jerusalem. Design and dimensions were all precisely noted, so that they might be perfectly recreated. Back home again, construction began. As a labor of love, the Upper Room was built almost entirely by volunteers. It was dedicated in a moving torch-light ceremony on July 4, 1982.

As ever, God was faithful to His word. The property mortgage note for Heritage USA was burned. A new era of growth was ushered in.

*Strolling along the avenue (**opposite**) at Heritage USA. Class in session (**above**) at Heritage Academy. The "Jim and Tammy TV Ministry Hour" (**following page**).*

The 25,000 square-foot Total Learning Center was built to accommodate the educational, spiritual and emotional needs of the rapidly expanding church congregation. Home of the Heritage Village Church Academy and the School of Evangelism and Communications, the new complex would also serve as headquar-

ters for the daily seminars, and for numerous workshops and conferences.

The main church complex was completed with the building and dedication of the new Broadcast Center in 1983, the first permanent home for the broadcasting arm of the church.

A friendly doorman welcomes all guests to the Heritage Grand (opposite). The Heritage Grand (above).

During 1983, Heritage USA welcomed over a million visitors, and the newly opened Heritage Inn could not begin to accommodate the ever-increasing throng. The sight of thousands of families coming to Heritage USA for spiritual refreshment and renewal, only to be turned away for lack of lodging, grieved Pastor Bakker's heart. He longed for an adequate fellowship center. In September of that same year he roughly sketched the concept that would eventually unfold as the master plan for the Heritage Grand Hotel or, as it should best be called, the Heritage Grand "Partner Center."

In November, ground was broken and in December, 1984, just over a year later, the seemingly impossible dream became a reality, with a live, nationally-telecast celebration that officially opened the 500 room Heritage Grand Partner Center...a beautiful place of lodging where Christians from all over the world from many religious backgrounds gather for fellowship. Here, the finest in inspirational music is heard, prayer meetings take place in the lobby, Bible seminars are taught several times a day, and even the morning wake-up call is a prayer.

Main Street Heritage USA.

The second phase of the Partner Center, the adjacent 21-story Heritage Grand Towers, begun in the spring of 1985, will offer 500 additional rooms, as well as shopping, recreational and dining facilities.

Current plans to minister better to the needs of Heritage Village Church members, residents and visitors include a medical center and total-life care facility for the elderly.

The proposed new Ministry Center, inspired by the Crystal Palace built in London in 1851, will house the new sanctuary for the rapidly-growing Heritage Village Church and will

(following page) Dining and Christian entertainment in the Grand Palace Cafeteria.

also provide Christian conference facilities for up to 30,000 people.

Pastor Bakker's over-all concept for a complete Christian community includes the development of a wide range of housing, offering a variety of accommodations. Together these make up one essential element of the total Christian living center. In this tranquil environment, both the young and the elderly, the family and the single person can live securely, can find renewal, and can know they are cared for and supported by the fellowship of their Christian neighbors.

107

Those coming to be ministered to at Heritage USA enjoy the beauty and peaceful comfort of the Heritage Grand *(above and left)*. The fellowship lobby at Christmas *(opposite)*.

*Fine dining in the Heritage Grand (**above**) and inspirational music (**below**) in the fellowship lobby.*

The church's singers and musicians **(top)** minister regularly along Main Street Heritage USA. Ye Olde Bookstore **(above)** and the Royal Hair Design **(right)**, both located on Main Street.

*Culinary delights abound in the Partner Center, from sumptuous buffets in the Heritage Grand lobby **(above)**, to Susie's Ice Cream Parlor on Main Street **(below)**.*

The Heavenly Fudge Shoppe offers delicious varieties of homemade fudge with warm, loving smiles.

Canoeing and paddle boating are available on the serene shores of Lake Heritage (above). Heritage Inn (below) offers comfortable accommodations amidst scenic beauty.

*Lakeside Chalets **(above and below)** provide the perfect setting for family enjoyment.*

121

*Heritage USA includes a varied selection of housing to meet the diverse needs of the congregation. Beautiful homes in Mulberry Village **(top)**, Wood Ridge **(left)** and Dogwood Hills **(right)** provide the security of living in a Christian community with the serenity of a natural setting.*

The spacious bedrooms (left) and wooden decks (right) of Mulberry Village. (below) The seven-story Mulberry Towers condominiums help meet the growing housing needs of the congregation.

*A*nd he saith unto them, Follow me, and I
will make you fishers of men.

MATTHEW 4:19 KJV

The Heritage Village recreational ministry provides a lively expression of God's love for the whole family. In a day when the evils around us are such a threat to the young, Heritage Village Church has determined that it will provide attractive facilities for an exciting environment of Christ-centered fellowship.

*Children delight in learning about animals
and nature at the parks and petting zoo
(right). Exploring the beauty of Heritage
USA on horseback (opposite & top).*

*Gospel music **(top)** at Buffalo Park. Pastor Bakker **(right)** with children at the playground in Buffalo Park. **(opposite)** One of Heritage USA's outdoor swimming pools, located on the shores of Lake Heritage.*

For the young and the young at heart *(above and right)* the colorful carousel in Recreation Village is one of the greatest delights at Heritage USA. *(opposite)* The Heritage Island inspirational water park provides, fun, recreation, live Christian music, refreshments and fellowship in a wholesome family atmosphere.

As we have therefore opportunity, let us do good unto all men, especially unto them who are of the household of faith.

GALATIANS 6:10 KJV

Getting from place to place at Heritage USA is an exciting adventure for the millions who visit the nearly four-square-mile retreat center. From the moment of arrival guests are efficiently served by a courteous transportation team. Whether singing praises or learning about the various ministry facilities, visitors enjoy fellowship while riding in the comfort of air-conditioned coaches, trams, double-decker buses and a quaint replica of the 1864 C.P. Huntington train.

*Double decker view and the C.P. Huntington train **(top)**. Air-conditioned coach buses and open air trams **(below)** transport partners through the church complex.*

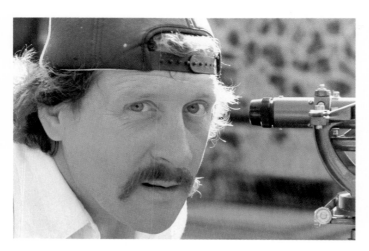

The church depends on the dedicated labor of skilled workers **(above)** to carry out the daily work of the ministry.

W*hy is it that he gives us these special abilities to do certain things best? It is that God's people will be equipped to do better work for him, building up the Church, the body of Christ, to a position of strength and maturity.*

EPHESIANS 4:12, TLB

Essential to the ministry of Heritage Village Church is the dedicated staff of trained workers who maintain and beautify the church facilities, assist with viewer communications, develop the latest technical and information systems, provide services to visitors, and help the vision to expand through building construction.

A trained team of technicians helps operate the studio video-editing equipment *(top)*, develop the Heritage Island water park *(above)*, and *(left)* maintain the church's computer information systems. *(below)* The church's security team serves the needs of the congregation and the community of Heritage USA.

Pastor and Mrs. Bakker host the daily "Jim and Tammy TV Ministry Hour."

I *am made all things to all men, that I might by all means save some.*

I CORINTHIANS 9:22 KVJ

Reaching beyond the borders of the Heritage Village Church, the *Jim and Tammy TV Ministry Hour* telecast penetrates into the homes and hearts of America with a heart-warming message of hope and unconditional love.

The program, produced daily and hosted by Jim and Tammy Bakker, broadcasts the encouraging word to millions that, no matter what the circumstances might be in their lives, they can "make it" with God's help.

Broadcast before a live congregation, the telecast features Christian music, dynamic testimonies, worship and faith-building messages. Guests include athletes, actors, authors, government leaders, evangelists, entertainers, businessmen and housewives...all testifying to the transforming power of God in their lives.

This broadcast ministry of the church extends into homes, hospitals, hotels and prisons, inviting viewers to call and receive ministry from trained phone counselors who are prepared to pray for the needs of this vast unseen congregation.

*Billy Graham (**above**) is interviewed by Jim and Tammy on the program set and Norma Zimmer (**left**) ministers in song.*

C.M. Ward

Robert Schuller

Oral Roberts

Rex Humbard

And daily in the temple, and in every house, they ceased not to teach and preach Jesus Christ.

ACTS 5:42 KJV

"We will have preaching and worship services here at Heritage USA every night until Jesus comes."

With that commitment, Pastor Bakker has carried on the legacy of the early revivalists.

Leading preachers, teachers, and evangelists from around the world share God's Word with the local and television congregations in camp-meeting, preaching and daily seminars.

Jimmy Clanton

Bob Gass

Rosey Grier

Charles Stanley

Dale Evans & Roy Rogers

Richard Roberts

Pat Boone

Gavin MacLeod

T.F. Zimmerman

Paul Yonggi Cho

Efrem Zimbalist, Jr.

Willard Cantelon

Jamie Charles and his father interview Art Linkletter.

Willa Dorsey

Donna Douglas

The Bakkers, James & Betty Robison, and other guests **(above)**. Howard & Vestal Goodman **(opposite)**.

Dean Jones

Kenneth Copeland

Andrae Crouch

Mike Warnke

Uncle Henry and Dick Wilson

Lisa Whelchel

Tammy Bakker interviews Mickey & Jan Rooney.

Pearl Bailey

Mother Angelica

The Bakkers have long been recognized as pioneers in Christian television, and since their earliest days in broadcasting, a team of faithful men and women has helped them to make this daily telecast one of the most powerful evangelistic outreaches of our time. Faithful and committed Christians, including beloved co-host Uncle Henry, have stood steadfast through the years, believing in the vision, and laboring unselfishly against seemingly insurmountable odds to continue broadcasting the salvation message until Christ returns.

Jim Bakker (above) converses with puppet guests Susie Moppet and Allie Alligator, while Doug Oldham (left) helps host a telecast. (opposite) Uncle Henry Harrison, beloved co-host of the "Jim and Tammy TV Ministry Hour."

Tammy Bakker, Mike Adkins and a newborn guest (above). Bob and Jeanne Johnson (opposite).

Jerry Clower

Carol Lawrence

Mike Murdock

Jim Hampton

Della Reese

Dave Boyer

This experienced and highly skilled group of producers, technicians, designers and writers prayerfully coordinate the elements of production in a format that is flexible yet always sensitive to the leading of God's Spirit. Essential to the program are the featured renditions of the PTL Orchestra and Singers, blended with the voices of the PTL Musical Family.

The *Jim Bakker* program was nationally syndicated in 1975 and is now telecast with its new title, the *Jim and Tammy TV Ministry Hour*, on more than 150 television stations throughout America. Presently, the broadcast saturates 95 percent of the continental United States and also reaches audiences in Canada, the U.S. Virgin Islands, Alaska and the Hawaiian Islands.

Doug Oldham (top) with the PTL Singers and Orchestra. Pastor Bakker in a pre-production meeting (left) and on the air (above) with Tammy, actress Kim Fields, and daughter Tammy Sue.

*And I saw another angel flying through the
heavens, carrying the everlasting Good News
to preach to those on earth—to every nation,
tribe, language and people.*

REVELATION 14:6 TLB

*Reviewing plans (**above**) in Satellite Valley. (**opposite**) A live telecast from the fellowship lobby of
the Heritage Grand.*

On April 3, 1978, with the dedication of PTL's satellite network, Pastor Jim Bakker proclaimed, "We have begun a broadcast that will not stop until Jesus returns."

This momentous occasion marked the advent of a new age in television technology and a new era of ministry and evangelism. The Heritage Village Church received the first private satellite license ever issued, and began broadcasting the Gospel 24 hours a day on the nation's premier satellite network.

Now, from its base in Satellite Valley at Heritage USA, *PTL—The Inspirational Network* transmits its satellite signal to more than 15 million homes. The network audience is increasing daily as PTL continues to expand its cable systems throughout the United States.

Part of PTL's vision to provide quality, 100 percent religious programming on *The Inspirational Network* includes the production of a wide spectrum of programs to meet the unique needs represented in the vast network audience. PTL has produced outstanding Christian programs such as *Sound Effects, Emotion Explosion, Camp Meeting USA* and many other PTL musical and informational specials.

Heritage USA Update, a fast-paced, informative program, was developed to keep those who support this ministry abreast of what it is accomplishing. The magazine format highlights the activities, services and outreaches of Heritage Village Church.

Tammy Faye ministers in song **(above)** *during the "Jim and Tammy TV Ministry Hour" and* **(opposite)** *interviews guests during her own daily program.*

A *merry heart doeth good like a medicine...*

PROVERBS 17:22 KJV

In addition to hosting the *Jim and Tammy TV Ministry Hour* telecast with her husband, Tammy Faye has provided her own delightful brand of programming over the years. A live audience, a wide range of guests, a festive atmosphere and Tammy's vivacious, spontaneous personality combined to create the popular and explosive "Tammy's House Party."

Moments from "Tammy's House Party" *(opposite and above)* and on location in California with popular television and motion picture actor, Mr. T *(below)*.

159

*Love...does not hold grudges and will hardly
even notice when others do it wrong.*

I CORINTHIANS 13:5 TLB

The heart of the ministry is never better exemplified than when our production crew captures Tammy ministering the love and hope of Jesus Christ behind prison walls. Her radiant message, heartfelt music and warm compassion offer a moment of hope for some, a new life for others who discover the liberating power of Jesus Christ.

*Tammy offers a message of hope to inmates (**left and below**) during her visits to the mens' and womens' prison facilities. (**opposite**) Listening compassionately to a prisoner's heartcry.*

*During his journey to the Holy Land, Pastor Bakker reports to the church congregation from the Upper Room **(left)** and plants trees with Tammy and friends **(right)** on a hillside in Israel.*

The PTL television crew often loads its camera gear and accompanies Pastor Bakker and Tammy as they minister across the nation and around the world. These ''on location'' productions have taken the team from prisoners to the President, from Hollywood to the Holy Land...thereby including the television congregation in some of the ministry's most significant moments.

162

Pastor Bakker reports from the ancient ruins of baths at Solomon's Temple in Jerusalem (above) and interviews Dr. David Lewis during a special program at Jerusalem's historic Wailing Wall (below).

During Pastor Bakker's memorable visit to Israel in 1981, the television viewers were able to experience the thrill of exploring the land of Christ's ministry. The programs originated from such hallowed landmarks as Calvary, the Mount of Olives, the Wailing Wall, and the Upper Room, where Jim carefully noted specifications for the replica that was soon thereafter to be built at Heritage USA.

A unique mission for the Heritage Village Church is the current restoration of the historical setting of Christ's crucifixion. After viewing the desecrated and neglected site in Jerusalem, Pastor Bakker was compelled to redeem and beautify Calvary and restore its dignity.

In 1983, PTL was selected as the official television network to cover the events of the National Convention of Religious Broadcasters (left) in Washington, D.C. The music of the PTL orchestra was featured at the convention and one of the highlights presented to the television audience was President Ronald Reagan's stirring address to the convention delegates.

*Pastor Bakker **(opposite)** offers the prayer at the official inaugural ceremony at the National City Church in Washington, D.C. during President Reagan's inauguration in 1981.*

The 1981 World Prayer Conference in Hawaii (below) was one of the most significant moments for the ministry. Hundreds of partners gathered from all corners of the globe to join with the church family in prayer and intercession. All of PTL's foreign program hosts were in attendance and brought delegations from many nations to this great prayer meeting. The PTL cameras documented this momentous event, and the *Jim Bakker* program originated from Honolulu during the conference.

Remote broadcasts have also been telecast from Christian Retreat in Bradenton, Florida, the General Council of the Assemblies of God in Anaheim, California, and the Christian Artists Seminar in Estes Park, Colorado. Tammy Faye has taped numerous interviews with Christian celebrities on location in California.

The cameras were present to capture the exciting moment at the 1985 Angel Awards in Los Angeles when Tammy Faye Bakker was awarded "Best Female Vocalist" for her album, "In The Upper Room." The ministry was the recipient of numerous awards for excellence in Christian television production.

*Tammy Faye (**opposite**) has recorded nearly two dozen albums and her daughter, Tammy Sue (**right**), is following in her mother's musical footsteps with her own contemporary music style. Tammy Faye Bakker (**left**) with the Angel Award bestowed on her by Religion in Media, which named her "Best Female Vocalist of the Year."*

The childhood home of Evangelist Billy Graham which has been relocated, reconstructed and refurbished as a historic landmark at Heritage USA.

Remove not the ancient landmark, which thy fathers have set.

PROVERBS 22:28 KJV

Jim Bakker recognizes that our modern "throw away" society is in danger of losing much of its valuable religious and cultural heritage. With the vital impact of religious heritage on his own life, Pastor Bakker determined that Heritage Village Church would preserve, promote and bring to life the heritage of our Christian faith and religious roots in America.

Pastor Bakker affirms, "We believe that many of the arts originated in the church, belong in the church, and should be revived within the church." Today, Heritage USA is fast becoming a Christian cultural center with inspirational musicals, drama and the fine arts.

Creation of the Heritage Society is helping to preserve historical landmarks of the Church and its art forms for all future generations.

Interior design and furnishings for the Graham Home have been carefully researched for accuracy and detail.

P*raise ye the Lord. Praise God in his sanctuary: praise him in the firmament of his power...Let every thing that hath breath praise the Lord. Praise ye the Lord.*

PSALM 150:1,6, KJV

Dramatic scene from Heritage Village Church's Christmas production, "Love Came Down" **(opposite).** *The Celebration Singers* **(above)** *carol on Main Street during the Christmas season.*

Dramatized in the outdoor setting of the Jerusalem amphitheater, the Heritage USA Passion Play depicts the miracles and ministry of Jesus Christ and is a moving presentation of sight and sound.

*An atmosphere of praise, worship and song pervades the Heritage Grand Ministry Center (**above and below**).*

*Praise and worship at the All-Night Gospel Sing in the sanctuary **(above)**. The Gospel is presented through drama and music at the Christian dinner theatre **(below)**.*

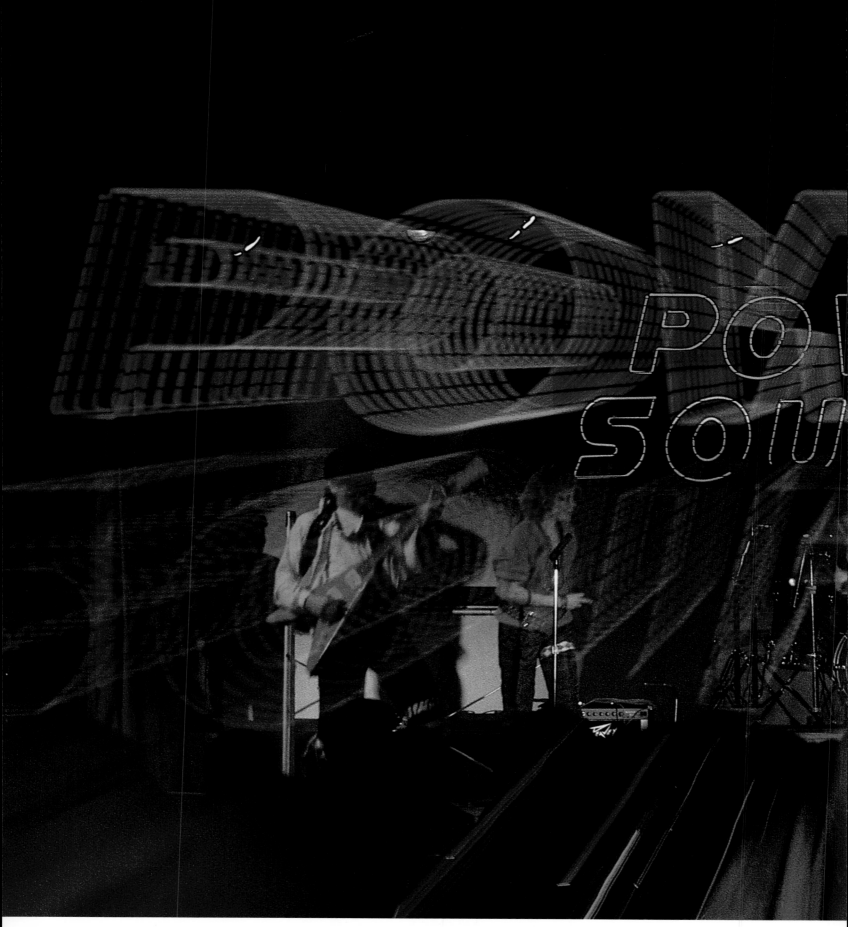

PowerSource, the youth outreach of Heritage Village Church, presents a series of Gospel concerts throughout the year expressly for the younger audience.

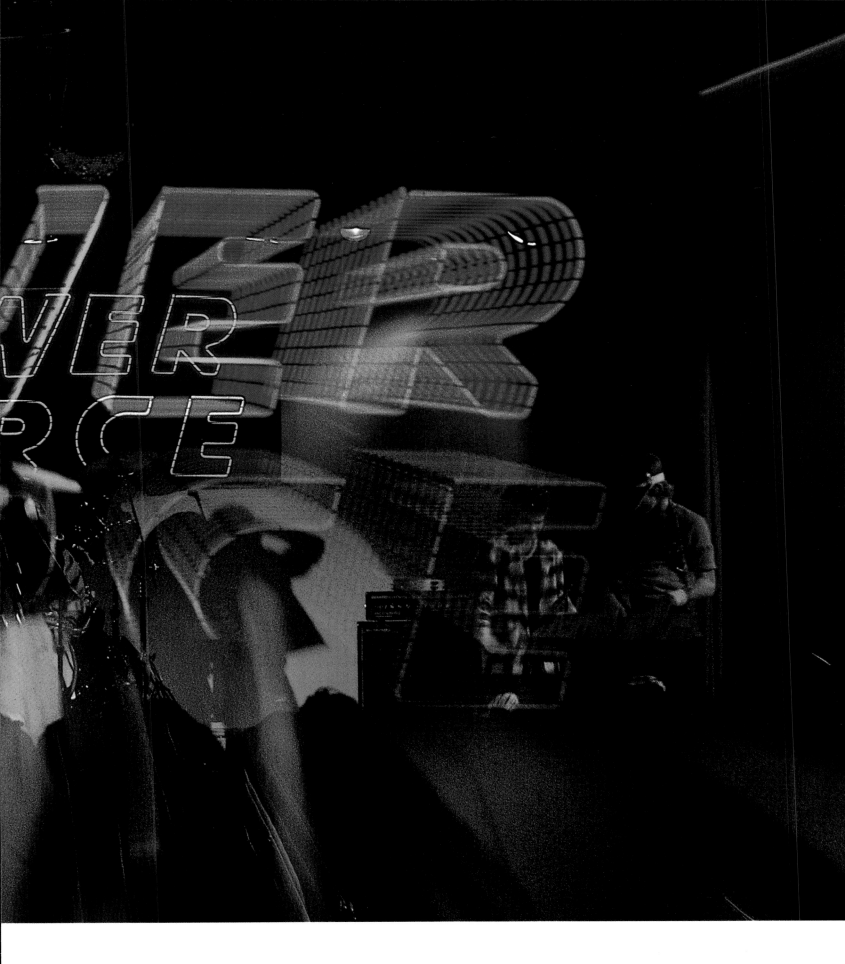

Pastor Bakker celebrates his birthday (above) with the television congregation. (opposite) Tammy celebrates the joy of Christmas in song.

During those celebration days each year you
must explain to your children why you are
celebrating—it is a celebration of what the
Lord did for you...

EXODUS 13:8 TLB

April 1, 1986 marked the 25th Anniversary of Pastor Jim and Tammy Bakker's ministry and marriage. To honor the Bakkers for their leadership and faithfulness, the congregation gathered together and expressed their love with a special Silver Anniversary banquet *(right)* followed by a Grand March down Main Street Heritage USA *(opposite)*. The Board of Directors *(below)* joins with hundreds of friends in praying for Jim and Tammy at the conclusion of the celebration.

In this age of secularism, Heritage Village Church offers Christmas City as a tribute to the true meaning of Christmas—the birthday of Christ. The biblical story is brought to life with the Living Nativity, with dramatic productions, avenues of lights, and sacred music and song. Thousands of visitors daily experience this stirring pageantry, presented by Heritage Village Church as a gift of love to our generation.

*An enchanting entranceway of lights **(below)** at Christmas City. The church choir **(opposite)** presents the annual "Living Christmas Tree" in the church sanctuary.*

Christmas City at Heritage USA.

*A delightful Christmas program **(above)** for children. **(below)** The wonder of Christmas reflected through the eyes of a child. **(opposite)** Singers celebrate the joy of Gospel music on New Year's Eve.*

The Welcome Center *(above)* at Christmas. *(below)* Pastor Bakker shares communion and a Christmas message. The Bakker family *(opposite)* at the New Year's Eve celebration.

*The congregation **(above)** celebrates God's great blessing of the Heritage Village Church during the New Year's Eve festivities. **(opposite)** The 10th Anniversary Victory Parade files past the reviewing stand as friends, visitors and church members commemorate the birth of the Heritage Village Church.*

T*his is the day which the Lord hath made; we will rejoice and be glad in it.*

PSALMS 118:24, KJV

July 4th, Independence Day, is doubly significant, commemorating the birth of our republic and the birth of our own Heritage Village Church. All day worship services with parades and fireworks are part of our "Passover," a time each year when we remember how God has miraculously delivered us from our enemies. This is a day of rejoicing throughout Heritage USA as we celebrate our heritage and the great victories won.

During the annual July 4th Victory Celebration (above and below), Heritage USA is alive with music, parades, ministry and fellowship. (opposite) Victory Day culminates with a dramatic fireworks display over the waters of Lake Heritage.

"I've traveled the world over and built churches in 47 states. I have never seen anything to compare with Heritage USA. As far as I'm concerned, it's the 'the eighth wonder of the world.'"
                                    —Roe Messner
            Builder of the world's largest churches.

The Dream Never Ends

*Enlarge your house; build on additions;
spread out your home! For you will
soon be bursting at the seams...*

ISAIAH 54:2 TLB

For Pastor Bakker and the congregation of the Heritage Village Church, the dream to build a worldwide, 21st century Christian retreat center is never ending.

Since its opening in 1978, Heritage USA has welcomed over 10 million visitors from all fifty states and many foreign nations. Men and women come to the church to be healed, refreshed and revitalized in a Christian environment unlike anything the world has ever known. Children flock to the recreational facili-

ties, the youth worship services, and the Family Center to meet new friends and enjoy life-changing experiences. The elderly who join the community of Heritage USA find a peaceful, secure and loving environment where they are able to feel a renewed sense of self-worth.

The Heritage Village Church continues to grow and expand at an unprecedented rate as families from across the nation restructure their lives to come and join the local church body.

With a burden for and a commitment to his

The Ministry Center will house the new sanctuary of the Heritage Village Church.

ever-expanding congregation, Pastor Bakker has unveiled his master plan for a total living center where the diverse needs of every segment of the congregation can be met.

The new Ministry Center at Heritage USA will house the church sanctuary which will be the largest in the world. Inspired by the famed Crystal Palace built in London in 1851, the one million square foot Ministry Center will feature a fully equipped 5,000 seat television studio, one hundred offices for counseling and special ministry needs, as well as hundreds of classrooms for daily Bible seminars and workshops.

The facilities in the Ministry Center will accommodate up to 30,000 people, meeting the local church's need, and also a worldwide need for a major Christian conference center.

For the thousands who come daily to worship at the Ministry Center, Pastor Bakker's

dream includes providing comfortable lodging in the peaceful, secure atmosphere of Heritage USA. The Crystal Tower will offer one, two and three-bedroom units on a time-share basis for guests and visitors to the Heritage Village Church. For those desiring to make Heritage USA their home, the seven-story Mulberry Towers will provide a selection of condominiums for the growing local community.

To awaken an appreciation and greater understanding of our historic Christian heritage, the church is recreating the streets of Old Jerusalem on the grounds of Heritage USA. Incorporating the existing Upper Room prayer center and the outdoor Jerusalem Amphitheatre, home of the Heritage Passion Play, Old Jerusalem will include the reproduction of many biblical historic sites and authentic style lodging facilities. Pastor Bakker's dream is to

The 21-story Heritage Grand Towers *(above)* offers comfortable rooms *(left)* , dining and fellowship facilities, and convenient access to the adjacent Heritage Grand Ministry Center. The Crystal Tower *(opposite)* will offer housing on a time-share basis for those coming to be ministered to at the new Ministry Center.

Located amidst the rural beauty of Farm Village, "Kevin's House" provides a godly home (below) and loving care for severely disabled children. Kevin Whittum (left), a wonderful young man with a giant-sized heart and spirit, helped inspire Jim Bakker to build the unique residence. (opposite) The streets of Old Jerusalem will be recreated at Heritage USA to awaken a greater understanding of historic Christian heritage.

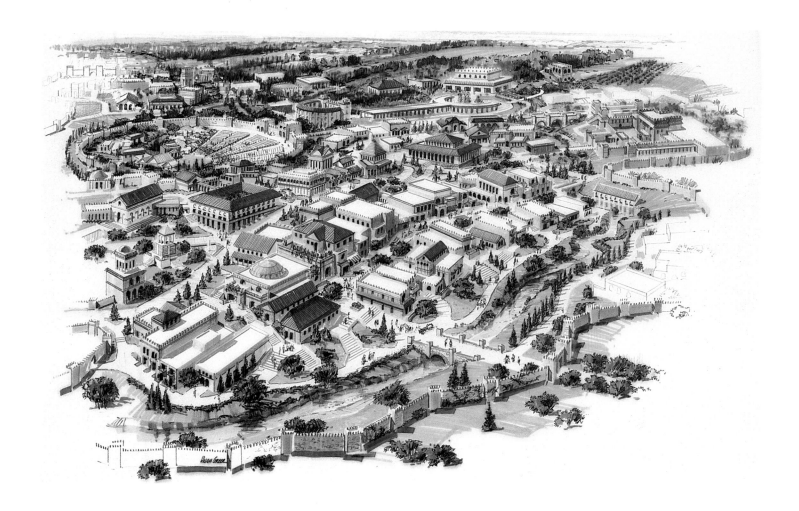

make Old Jerusalem an unforgettable cultural and spiritual experience for every visitor who has yearned to explore the land of the Bible.

For the elderly who are dependent on the help of others, the community of Farm Village is a dream come true. Quaint homes, small gardens and pleasant dining facilities will be nestled among rolling meadows and flowing creeks to provide an invigorating atmosphere for those restricted by age and health difficulties.

On the edge of Farm Village stands "Kevin's House," a beautiful, Victorian-style home that provides loving foster care in a family environment for severely disabled children who would otherwise be institutionalized. For these children, the nightmare of desertion has dissolved into a dream fulfilled as they discover their unique purpose as God's special creation.

Pastor Bakker's dream continues as his heart is burdened for the young and the elderly, for the lonely and the hurting, for the fractured families and the abandoned men and women of our society. As long as there is one more marriage to be saved, one more senior citizen who needs to be loved, or one more deserted child who needs to know God loves him, the vision is not in vain.

For Pastors Jim and Tammy Bakker and the Heritage Village Church, the dream never ends.

This, then, is Heritage Village Church, one member of the church universal that is the Body of Christ, the fellowship of all true believers.

Our devotion, our mission, our purposes are those of the Christian Church throughout the ages. We hold all those who love Christ to be our family. Here, and at the farthest limits of our reach, now and as long as we shall be given the strength, we shall carry out Jesus' command, *"Thou shalt love the Lord thy God with all thy heart, and with all thy soul, and with all thy mind. This is the first and great commandment. And the second is like unto it, Thou shalt love thy neighbor as thyself. On these two commandments hang all the law and the prophets."*

MATTHEW 22:37-40 KJV

There are three things
that remain—faith, hope, and love—
and the greatest of these is love.

I CORINTHIANS 13:13, TLB